MW01631264

# AND THE MAGICAL BEARPLANE™

JONATHAN GUNSON
WRITER & ILLUSTRATOR

RICHARD ROBINSON
ILLUSTRATOR

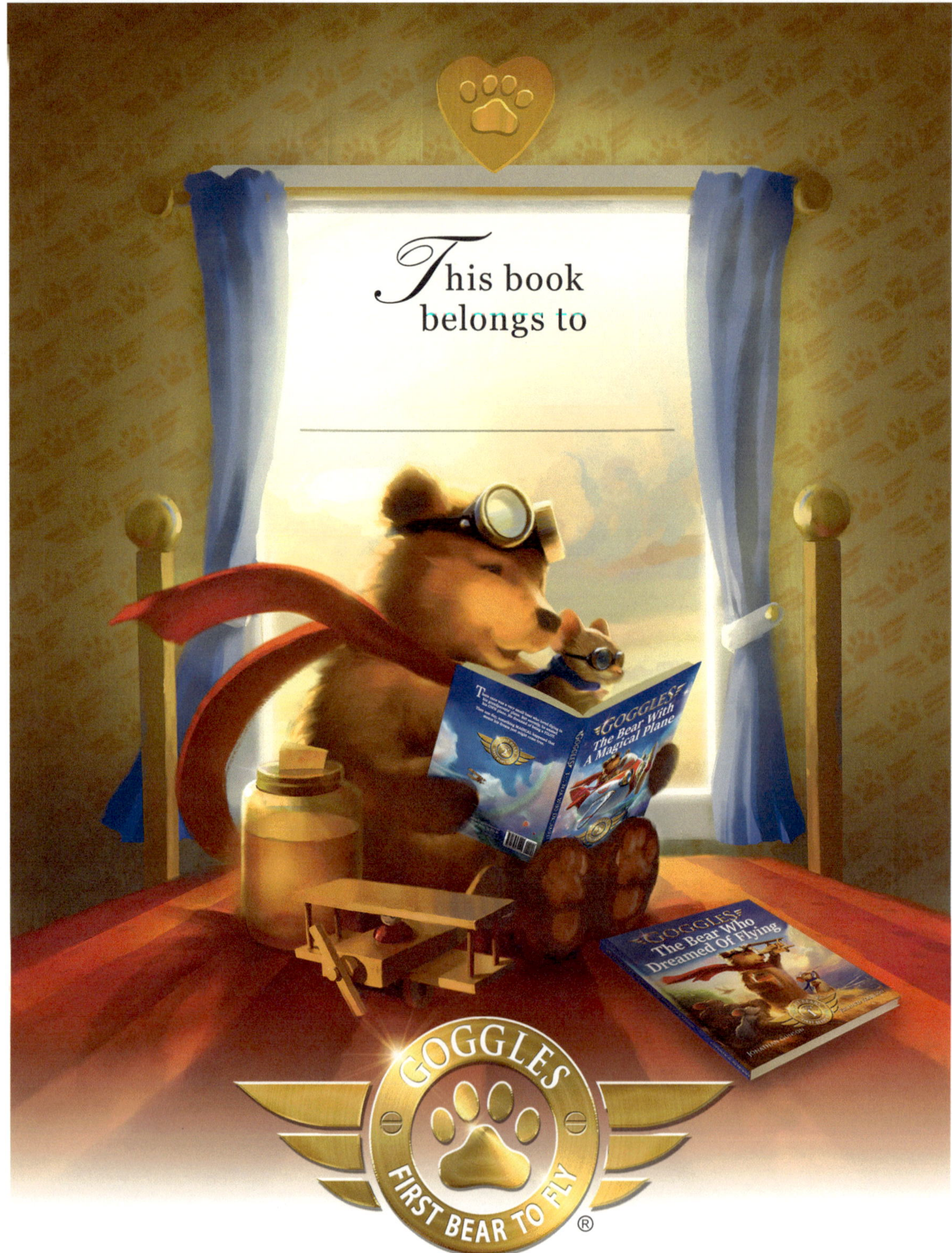


© Copyright 2022 Creative World Limited (New Zealand)

All rights reserved. No part of this book may be reproduced, transmitted, or stored in an information retrieval system in any form or by any means, graphic, electronic, or mechanical, including photocopying, audio or visual recording, without prior written permission from Creative World Ltd (NZ Company).

Trademarks: Goggles Flying Bear® First Bear To Fly® Wright Bears™ Bearplane™

ISBN 978-0-473-53442-4

Written by Jonathan Gunson

Illustrations by Richard Robinson
& Jonathan Gunson

This is Goggles, the flying bear. He loves to fly so much, he wears flying goggles wherever he goes.

Goggles and his grandparents, Growlville & Wilma Wright, were the first bears to fly. They built the honey-powered 'Wright Flyer' airplane.

Goggles loved flying with his grandparents as they soared around the clouds doing skywriting, looping-the-loop, and candy bombing.

But secretly, he wanted to fly his OWN plane. He dreamed of being a PILOT.

HONEY

On Goggles' birthday, Grandpa took him to the toy store.
He had a surprise waiting. Can you guess what it was?

TOYS & MAGIC

A toy airplane, that could really fly!

"It's a Bearplane!" shouted Goggles.
"It's the fastest ever, and has water bombs!" said Mr Rabbit, the store owner. "Let's fly it outside," said Grandpa. But Goggles couldn't wait. He pushed the 'GO' button.

The Bearplane took off and raced around the toy store.

But then it flew straight into the magic display, which exploded in a cloud of enchanted stardust.

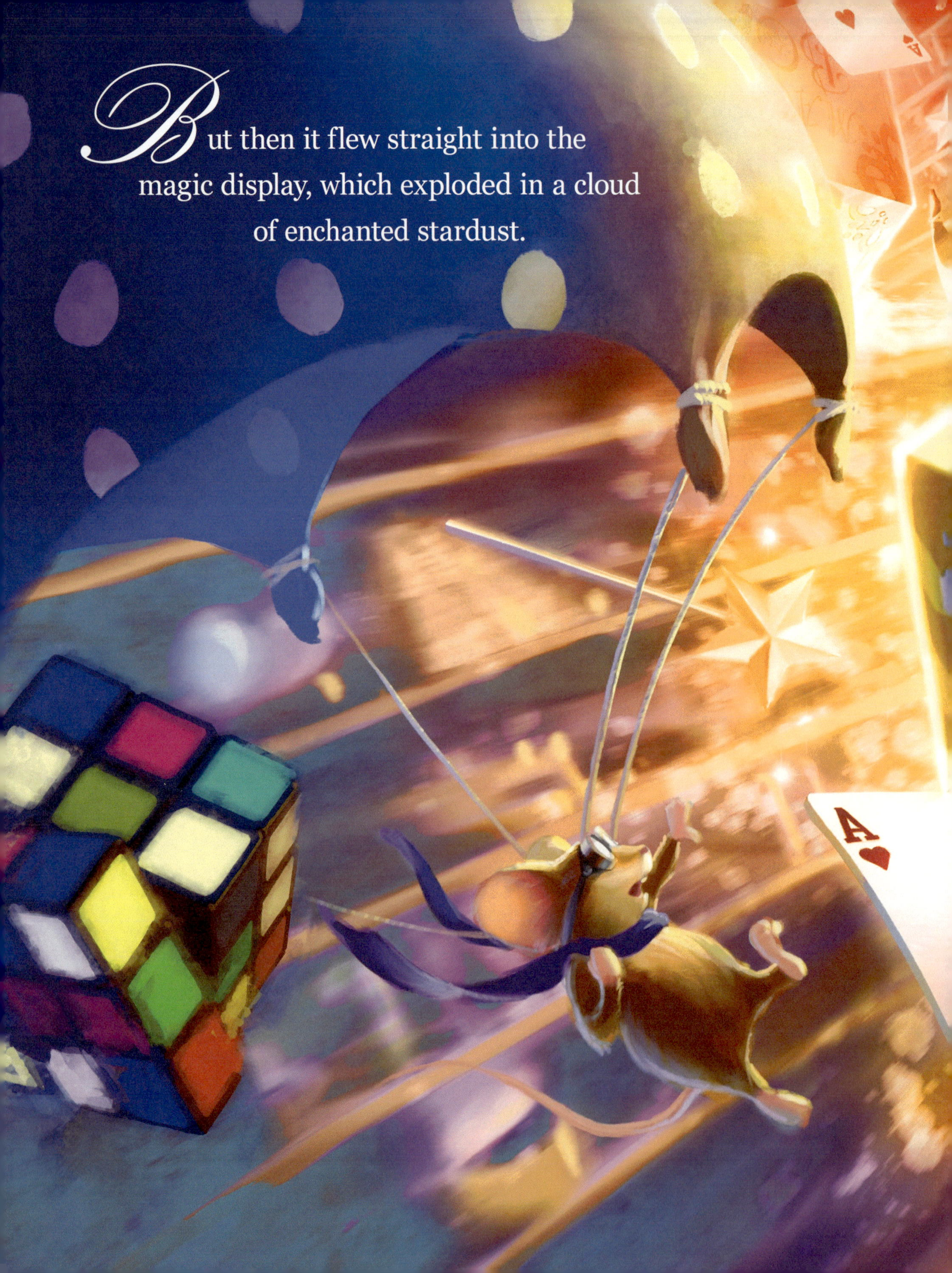

KABOOM!
MAGIC BOX

"Whooooo!" said Mr Rabbit,
"Something strange has happened to your plane."
The Bearplane floated in front of them,
sparkling mysteriously.

It's magical!

Back at home, Goggles was very sad. If he couldn't fly a toy plane, how would he ever fly a real one? He'd NEVER be a pilot.

To cheer him up, Grandma found him a jar of his favorite honey. But ... she almost dropped it.

"I'm so tired," she said. "Cats keep yowling outside my bedroom window and I can't get a wink of sleep."

Now Goggles felt even more sad, he was worried about Grandma.

Late that night, Goggles was woken by a tinkling sound in his bedroom.

The Bearplane had grown to full size, and the pilot's door swung open for him.

Goggles climbed into the cockpit.

"Welcome aboard," said the Bearplane. "Where would you like to fly?"

"I'd like to save Grandma from the cats," said Goggles. "Wonderful plan. Let's save the Gran!" said the Bearplane.

Goggles pushed the
'GO' button.

With a whizz and a whirr, the propeller began to spin.
The Bearplane lifted off and glided out the window.

Soon Goggles was flying high over the village. He could see all the tiny houses, far below.

Grandma's bedroom light was still on, even though it was late at night.

Two ragged cats strutted along the fence outside Grandma's window.

"She's trying to sleep again," sniggered one.

"Let's wake her up!" snickered the other.

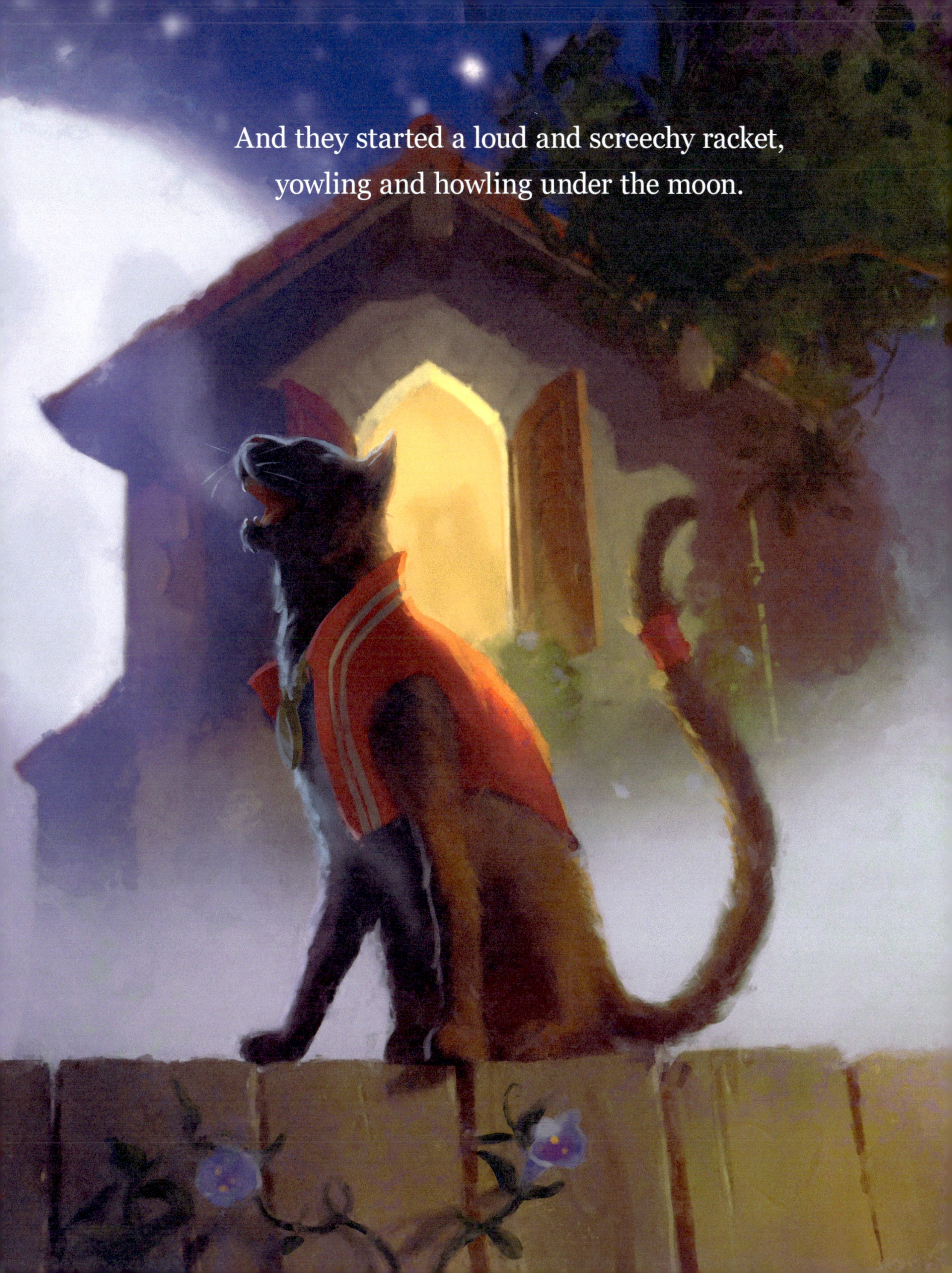

And they started a loud and screechy racket,
yowling and howling under the moon.

WATER

Goggles flew over the cats and pushed the 'Water Bomb' button. The bomb doors opened.

SPLOOSH!

The light went out in Grandma's window.

Goggles chased the cats all the way to the edge of the village,
then flew quietly back to his bedroom,
humming a little tune.

Everything was peaceful in the Wright Bears' house.

In the morning, the Bearplane had turned back into a toy.

"I had a lovely sleep last night," said Grandma Wilma. "The cats stopped yowling; I wonder why?"

But Goggles just smiled to himself. He was a REAL pilot now, and it was his secret.

# The Amazing Story of the FIRST 'Candy Bomber'

## US Airforce Pilot First Lieutenant Gail Halvorsen

US Airforce Pilot
First Lieutenant Gail Halvorsen

Douglas C-54 'Candy Bomber' arrives
at Templehof airfield, Berlin.

In 1948, US pilot Gail Halvorsen flew food supplies each day to people trapped in the city of Berlin by a Soviet blockade. The children were starving, so he began to drop candy from his plane.

Crowds of children waited each day for the 'Candy Bomber' to arrive, and they soon had more candy than they'd ever dreamed. Gail Halvorsen became famous as 'The Berlin Candy Bomber'.

Photographs courtesy of Colonel Gail Halvorsen. Utah, USA

Berlin children meet the 'Candy Bomber'.

GOGGLES™
Loves
Honey Bees
Nature's Royal Family

# Honey bees live together as a family in a large warm home called a beehive.

Forager bees hunt for flowers with pollen and nectar, and others make honey from the nectar. They are led by the Queen Bee, which makes them a truly royal family.

The Queen lays over 1000 eggs each day to grow her family. Nurse bees feed her and the babies (called Larvae) with 'royal jelly' made from pollen.

Bees make so much honey, there's plenty for humans as well.

GOGGLES™
AND THE MAGICAL BEARPLANE™
COLORING BOOK
GOGGLES
FIRST BEAR TO FLY
HONEY
GOGGLES®
FIRST BEAR TO FLY®

# FREE COLORING PAGES!

Get this whole book *'Goggles and the Magical Bearplane'* as coloring pages and enjoy it all over again!

FREE AT THIS WEBSITE:

**www.colorbook.fun**

Made in United States
Troutdale, OR
09/15/2023